Not in the plan.

A collection of poems about mental illness, childhood trauma, eating disorders and child to parent abuse.

Claire Hirst

BookLeaf Publishing

Not in the plan. A collection of poems about mental illness, childhood trauma, eating disorders and child to parent abuse.

Presentation by *BookLeaf Publishing*

Web: www.bookleafpub.com

E-mail: info@bookleafpub.com

ISBN: 9789357211864

First edition 2023

DEDICATION

For my husband, there’s no one else I want travel through the storm with.

ACKNOWLEDGEMENT

Thank you to my husband, Graham. He has remained faithful, supportive and strong throughout what has been and continues to be an immensely difficult journey and undoubtedly I would not be able to do this without him. He has tirelessly read and edited my poems despite not really being a poetry lover for which I am extremely grateful.

My daughter Sophie designed the artwork for the cover of this book. She is only fifteen, but is such a talented artist. I am so proud to have her work on the front of my book and it makes it all the more special. I am very grateful to her for letting me use it.

I also want to thank Dr Clare Cribb. She has been my psychotherapist for the past year and a half and has supported me throughout many difficult times, listened patiently and validated how I have felt. She has worked hard to allow me to feel less ashamed about having a mental illness and that sometimes things that happen to us are not our fault. She is an inspiration and has helped me to overcome some of my self-doubt in order to even publish this book, by helping me believe that my poems were good enough to be read by others.

It is during challenging times that we learn who our true friends are as they are the ones that remain with us though the hard times. I want to thank my longstanding friends. Alex and Jeanette who have been through so much of this with me as our children grew up together. Often offering a listening ear, plenty coffee, tissues and cwtches (hugs). Caroline and Rebecca who were both initially two great work colleagues but more recently have become so much more than that. Despite the challenge of staying in touch whilst I have been off work, they have remained dedicated to finding time initially meeting over a firepit in lockdown for a few glasses of wine. I am so grateful to them for continuing to make the effort and for not shying away from me because they didn't know how to react to my mental illness, unlike so many others. I also want to thank my longest standing friend Melissa who helped me through so many of my teenage years and probably was what allowed me to keep going all those years ago for so long. Although we don't see each other so much due to the distance I know I could count on her for anything and when we do see each other it is just like old times.

I also need to thank my parents. My late Mum who despite being critical was generous and caring also and my Dad who is incredibly intelligent, logical, and driven. He worked so hard to be able to provide financially for us all so that we never had to go without like he did as a child. Lastly, I am grateful to my children for providing me with such vast life experience and changing my life in so many ways. I won't deny it has been hard but it has given me greater insight into other people and taught me never to judge anyone else as you don't know what anyone else is going through. They have prompted me to reflect on my own childhood and have provided much inspiration for this book.

PREFACE

I didn't choose poems, poems chose me. When I was at my darkest moments my thoughts came in rhymes. Thick and fast. That's how it started.

I never planned to write poems. I was, am, a doctor. That is what I had always wanted to be. That is how my life was meant to be. But then I didn't plan on mental illness. Despite having had an eating disorder for 20 years I had hidden it from everyone including my husband. I didn't even see it as a mental illness myself most of the time. In medical school I knew I desperately needed help. However, the fear of showing weakness and anyone knowing meant that I would be found out. Support was minimal for mentally ill doctors at the time and even now stigma still exists. In my mind, I was certain I would be thrown out of University, and my life long dream of being a doctor lost forever. So, I remained hidden and suffered in silence. I graduated, got a job, married and had children. Things were going as planned and my career was progressing well. Life then, however, became progressively more difficult and after many years of struggles one of my children was diagnosed with high functioning Autism, ADHD and oppositional defiant disorder. As he grew older the challenges grew ever more difficult. At the same time there were challenges in work and the demands of a stressful job, a difficult work environment and juggling a child with additional unpredictable needs contributed to a decline in my mental health.

I went through a relentless period of depression and anxiety, had to stop working and at worse felt suicidal for prolonged periods. I also had to deal with my own childhood wounds from some difficult and painful experiences that I had suppressed along with dealing with the fall out of my eating disorder secret being revealed and my mother dying after a rapid unexpected 6 month illness with aggressive peritoneal cancer. Along with this I was repeatedly exposed to parent abuse from my child due to his challenging behaviour. My recovery journey has been fluctuating and inconsistent and I currently remain unfit to resume work as a doctor.

Over the past 2 years I have written poems on many of the things I have experienced as a way of coping with what I have been dealing with. I have found inspiration and comfort in reading the words of others experiencing similar things to me. They have helped me to feel less alone in my darkest moments.

The start of the book consists mainly of poems related to depression and the feelings I had about not being believed and being a failure and a burden and how it feels to feel that like is not worth living any longer. Following this are a collection of poems dealing with eating disorders, self-perception, conflicting emotions, and at the end a section on the roller coaster of emotions experienced whilst caring for a child that has challenging behaviour.

I hope that this book can help to reduce the stigma of mental illness. I hope that they can be words of comfort to others who may be experiencing similar challenges and feelings allowing them to feel understood and less alone in what may be a time of immense darkness.

Looking in from the Outside

You can't possibly be depressed
You have the perfect life
You own a nice big home
And have no financial strife

Your parents never got divorced
You were always clothed and fed
As a child lived in a house
With a warm and cosy bed

You went to university
To obtain a good degree
Your parents gave you money
Never had to beg or plea

You had a successful job
No problems to pay a bill
I'm sure that anyone else
For a life like yours would kill

Your husband is so loyal
Devoted to family and to you
He's hardworking and caring
Many other positive traits too

You're not repeatedly beaten
Nor are you addicted to drugs
You don't live in a rough area
Where you're scared or surrounded by thugs

You have a delightful garden
Packed full of beautiful flowers
Where you can listen to the birds
Or watch the sunset for hours

Adventures to countries abroad
Amazing places that you have been
Numerous wonderful things
You're so privileged to have seen

Your children both look well
And superficially seem happy enough
So, what is it in your life
That make it really so tough?

There's nothing that you can want
Certainly, that's how it does appear
To those looking in from the outside
And even those that you hold dear

People surrounding you only notice
That everything seems fine
Except maybe that you do drink
Possibly, a little too much wine

Even you can't comprehend
With everything that you've got
Why were you previously ok
But now you are patently not

"Look at everything she has"
I'm sure that's what people say
"No way can she be depressed"
"How on earth can she feel that way!"

Depression isn't something you choose
Feeling broken inside like this
Consumed with an emptiness
You're continually trying in vain to dismiss

Imagining people think you're a fraud
Doubtful, that you are believed
With the external projection conveyed
Of everything you have achieved

How can I possibly be mentally ill?
I was always feisty and strong
Like a flash a realisation hits hard
In reality, what if I was wrong?

It's not the things that you have
Or the things that you have done
Mental illness doesn't discriminate
Unpredictable, can happen to anyone

Happiness

Never take for granted
The things that make you smile
Pause to enjoy them
At least for a while

A walk near the ocean
Along a beautiful bay
Spotting a magical sunset
At the end of the day

Camping outside
On a crisp clear night
As the stars shine above
So dazzlingly bright

The crackle of logs
As you sit by a roaring fire
Sensing the thrill of adventure
As you fly down a zip wire

Laughing with friends
So hard until you cry
Feeling so invincible
You never want to die

What if one day you notice
Happiness just isn't there?
And living life without it
Is just so hard to bear?

It doesn't register at first
You've had unhappy days before
It's bound to be back soon
Of that you feel sure

After a while though, you realise
It doesn't start to return
Concern begins to mount
Is it something you have to relearn?

So, you make a conscious effort
Do things that brought joy before
Except, now they feel empty
There's a numbness you deplore

Maybe you have changed
So, you try something new
Desperately hoping that
Some enjoyment it brings to you

But, it's like it's been turned off
By the flick of a switch
Is it a brain malfunction?
A happiness software glitch?

No matter what you do
The emptiness won’t go away
Without happiness there's only
Despair and dismay

Now, as I sit in the garden
Listening to the birds sing
I miss the feeling of joy
That it previously did to bring

I still hope that one day
I will feel happiness again
But for now, I’ll just have to
Somehow, live without it until then

The Darkness Within

A feeling of being totally controlled
Every minute of every day
The constant needs and demands
Are making me fade away

Unaware it was even possible
To feel so dead inside
Seems impossible now to believe
That I ever felt alive

To wake each day is hard
When you wish that you weren't here
A struggle to go on another day
Let alone another year

Desperate to feel something other
Than emptiness, fear and dread
Like joy, happiness and excitement
Instead of deep longing for my bed

I put on my happy mask
To hide my daily pain
The reality is it's an act
Though it helps me to hide my shame

The smile can be convincing
But sadly, not the eyes
The windows into the soul
Struggle to keep up the disguise

Their sparkle and shine have gone
Now, they have a vacant stare
Caused by intolerable suffering
That is so hard to continue to bear

Emotions not easy to control
Can't hide it now when I cry
Feeling embarrassed and ashamed
Pride and dignity have waved goodbye

It's like I'm screaming in a vacuum
The noise is deafening to my ears
Yet no one else can hear my screams
They only see my hopeless tears

Why can't I make them hear?
Why can't I make them see?
How desperate I am inside
They only look straight through me

Before the darkness appeared
I was successful, passionate and free
Now I feel I have lost everything
I wonder why this happened to me

I try to ignore negative voices
Of the demons that live in my head
Tormenting me that nobody likes me
That everyone wishes I was dead

I endeavour to fight against the darkness
That now resides deep within
So tired, I'm losing the fight
Sometimes, I think it might even win

The Depression Robber

There's a robber on the loose
And he's going to take from you
Everything you loved
And everything you knew

He's taken your ability
To control how you feel
You therefore start to wonder
What else is he going to steal?

He's made it so that you
Can no longer go to work
Round dark corners you are certain
He does begin to lurk

Next, he drains your energy
From right in front of your eyes
There wasn't even time
To say any goodbyes

Your appetite is missing
No longer enjoyment of food
Happiness has been stolen
All that's left is despondent mood

Gone is your independence
Not trusted to be on your own
Demolished happy emotions
Turning your heart to stone

Next, he robs your family
And your ability to be a mum
You wonder to yourself
From where did this evil come?

Once, you were a good friend
But now you can't engage
Withdrawn, all you're left with
Is anger, hatred and rage

Married for so many years
As a wife were loyal and caring
But now that you have changed
Does your husband regret his life sharing?

Sleeping becomes so difficult
Broken slumber, often awake
Wishing to be unconscious
Just to give your brain a break

Cognitive function slow and sluggish
Thoughts stolen from your brain
To everyone who loves you
You're certain you're a total drain

No longer able to focus
Can't concentrate to drive
And then comes the worst part
Threatened is your instinct to survive

Gone is your self esteem
And all of you self worth
Then he takes your desire
To want to live on this earth

You try in vain to find replacements
For all the things you have lost
To have them back you would give anything
No matter what the cost

But money can't replace them
That's what you do discover
Unfortunately, these are things
No insurance policy will cover

Slowly, you start to fight back
Reluctantly, he begins to retreat
But then he makes another attack
He will never admit defeat

Elusive, you can never catch him
Best efforts will always fail
Because he's all around you
He can never be put in jail

Just leave, you remorseless thief
Why do you have to stay?
I just want my old life back
In every single way

There's nothing left now to take
All that remains is an empty shell
Hollow and alone
Stuck in a darkness hell

Burden

When I look at my husband
I see the strain in his eyes
The emotional burden I’ve become
Once again, my tears he dries

This time for what feels like
The twentieth time in a day
Depression has changed us both
In every single way

I notice the resentment
For the wife who's no longer there
As now onto his shoulders
Falls most of the care

At first he found it easier
When I did disconnect
I cried less and I looked
Less emotionally wrecked

Unpredictable as the weather
Sometimes I don’t want to be on my own
But other times for no reason
I’m desperate to be alone

Struggling, we schedule time
To try to reconnect
But if he changes his mind
I feel such a reject

If no longer wanted
Why fight to stay alive?
I question whether I really
Want to even survive

Until death do us part
We vowed and do believe
So now he is stuck
Therefore he cannot leave

Unable to trust me alone
But he needs some space
Feeling utterly drained
Tension shows on his face

Extremely sorry for him
Remorseful for all he's been through
If only we could go back
To the good times that we once knew

My son doesn't understand
Often asking "Is mummy alright?"
Wanting to cuddle all the time
And hold me so tight

Touch can be uncomfortable
Induces anxiety as well
Impulsive reaction when others too close
Like oil and water I physically repel

There are so many demands
"I want you to play!"
He can't comprehend
It's too difficult to do today

Motivation is at rock bottom
I just feel far too low
Irately in a tantrum
He will stormily go

My daughter is growing up
Gaining independence as a teen
She wants to be heard
And needs to be seen

I try hard to listen
But it's difficult to stay on track
My mind keeps on wandering
And I can't bring it back

When she returns home
I am normally in bed
Often far too exhausted
Or just stuck in my head

I try to appear normal
So, I put on an act
But sometimes it shows through
Then full of guilt am wracked

The darkness is stopping me
Be the mother they deserve
I worry of damage I am causing
To their future mental reserve

No longer able to work
So I'm on long term leave
Work colleagues don't keep in touch
I'm unimportant to them, I believe

I used to sit in my office
Alone, crying on the floor
Clearly evident that I
Couldn't take it any more

Unsupported and isolated
I would often sit and think
Are they even aware
That I am on the brink?

Managers talk about capability
"Will you ever return?"
Financial burden to my family
As now no money I earn

To my family I can see
They wish I was as before
It’s hard to watch someone fade
Who you previously used to adore

Truth

Don't ask how I am
If you only want me to say
That everything is great
And I feel wonderful today

When the reality is
That my life feels quite tough
And very often recently
I feel that I've had enough

I often feel lonely
That I'm all on my own
Can be surrounded by people
But still feel utterly alone

Emotionally overwhelmed
Anxiety that just won't subside
A hypervigilant state
That's so hard to abide

Every comment overanalysed
Brain sabotages what I think
As it focuses on the worst
My self-esteem starts to sink

Things that you've lost
Trigger feelings of grief
Often seems never ending
Like you'll never have relief

You don't choose to feel this
No desire to be so low
Want to be content within yourself
But the progress is slow

Don't try to fix me
Or tell me that I'll be okay
That life isn't that bad
Because it's all such a cliché

I don't need your advice
Telling me I shouldn't feel like this
Simply invalidates me
And my feelings does dismiss

I only need you to listen
With a sympathetic ear
And perhaps offer a tissue
If from my eye, slides a tear

I just want to feel seen
For you to acknowledge my pain
To know how I feel matters
Strong our friendship will remain

Please loan me your strength
If I'm feeling weak
Maybe give me a hug
To make the world feel less bleak

However, if you don't understand
Well, that's alright too
You've not walked in my shoes
Been through what I've been through

So, if that's the case
It's fine just to say
Can't imagine how it feels
Fortunately, I've never felt that way

Therefore, next time only ask
If you honestly want to know
I don't want to lie or be fake
So, my real feelings may show.

Impossible to Contemplate

It is hard to believe anyone else
Could possibly think this way
Or even begin to understand
You don't want to live another day

It's almost impossible to contemplate
Others are able to feel this low
But somehow carry on with life
Yet manage not to let it show

Sometimes I look at strangers
As they hurry on their way by
To see if I can spot
A certain look deep in their eye

Perhaps a glazed vacant stare
That says they've had enough
Everyday feels truly unbearable
Because things are just too tough

There is a stigma in feeling this way
So, we keep thoughts hidden well
Find unhealthy ways to cope
That become our own forms of hell

Everything feels desperately futile
Painfully, feels we're stuck this way now
Melancholy, is your new normal
You try to adjust to it somehow

But what if it's simply not enough
Memories taunt you from life before
Certainly, it wasn't all perfect
But alive, you felt so much more

Previously, you had some worth
Combined with confidence and pride
Something you wanted to live for
Now, there's only a self you can't abide

Disheartened and utterly useless
Your existence merely a bind
Sometimes not waking tomorrow
Perhaps might feel the least unkind

Closer towards the Brink

Thoughts of killing myself
Flood into my brain each day
And the reasons seem to diminish
Of why I should continue to stay

Detached feelings from everyone
Blur the way my brain does think
As I drift further away from them
And closer towards the brink

The lack of a close connection
Feeling a burden to them all
I don't know how to get past it
Like I'm hitting a solid brick wall

Nothing I do ever seems right
I feel I only ever make things worse
And for them living with me
Must be like being placed under a curse

Thoughts of dying have been there before
Coming and going like waves in the sea
But now they're accompanied by urges
A visceral feeling that's starting to scare me

When tension rises in the house
To hide in my bedroom, I do creep
But I can't hide from the noise and the stress
It's there, an urge from the window to leap

Or after an argument with my husband
And the feeling we're falling apart
The strain evident now in our marriage
The urges yet again they start

To take a handful of pills
To go to sleep and never awake
The temptation feels greater than ever
And so very difficult to shake

Although, that would take too long
I don't want a slow drawn out death
A time to change my mind
Feeling regret as I draw my last breath

Each time the feeling is there
I wonder will this time I give in
Will I go through with it eventually
Will I find the courage within?

Because I'm sick of living like this
No joy and no hope of reprieve
A feeling that nothing will improve
For the old me I can only grieve

Sometimes I wish I'd had the guts
To end it and now be at peace
To no longer feel anguish and pain
To feel calm and finally release

Each day feeling I barely exist
And the dread of being alive
I thought the normal human instinct
Was one of wanting to survive

But there must be a tiny part of me
That must want to make it through
But the storm just seems so vast
And it feels so incredibly hard to do

When I look at the path straight ahead
I see how difficult things will continue to be
Do I make the decision to keep being tortured
Like choosing the fires of hell that are right in
front of me?

I can't understand how nothing now matters
How can I no longer really care?
About things that were important before
Like my kids and wanting their lives to share

I always wanted to see them achieve
See what they turned out to be
Find a partner or maybe get married
Be there for times when they needed me

I had dreams I shared with my husband
Places I so wanted to see
I wanted to travel the world
Amazing places such excitement within me

Sometimes I wonder if I will still be here
Will I see the end of the year?
Will I make it to my next birthday?
Nothing now feels very clear

I don't make plans far in the future
Because I know them I might not be able to keep
I might have finally given in to the darkness
And have entered my never ending sleep

Asking for Help

I think I could do it
No word of a lie
This time feels different
I think I could die

I'm not really sure
But don't leave me alone
Suicidal feelings
Won't pick up the phone

And please don't ask me
If I will be ok
Because all I will tell you
Is you don't need to stay

Perhaps I am wrong
The pain is so raw
I've got so many pills
Over in my draw

I'm sure I could take them
And just fall asleep
As I lay in my bed
And continue to weep

But then you see me
Can tell I am not right
Then lie next to me
And hold me so tight

You tell me you need me
That we will get through
You are my rock
And I really trust you

You phone the secretary
Of the consultant I see
He is in clinic
Busy as can be

She'll discuss it with him
But don't hold your breath
Then you explain
Might be life or death

You ask her to call you
Just so we know
What else to do
Or where else to go

There is no call back
An opportunity missed
Feels like they don't care
One less on their list

You don't give up on me
You call the GP
They are fantastic
Support and refer me

Community mental health
That's who it is to
But over the phone
Is how they'll assess you

All because of Covid
There's no face to face
Clearly, it's too risky
They claim that's the case

You can go to the hairdresser
Or visit a shop
But direct patient contact
The NHS must stop

Even in a crisis
You still can't be seen
You have to be contacted
Over a screen

You might be at risk
You know you're in danger
It's difficult though
To tell a complete stranger

Your story you need
To frequently repeat
It's starting to feel
A lot like defeat

Eventually they'll decide
Your risk of dying
If they don't accept you
Perhaps you are lying?

If you convince them
They might take you on
But then if you don't
It's back to square one

My Teenage Self

Today I met myself
When I was just fifteen
I was young and innocent
And still very keen

It was like glimpsing
The ghost of Christmas past
Time seems to have flown by
So incredibly fast

Discovering my diary
From nearly 30 years ago
What struck me most was
There was no warm glow

My diary was my best friend
For so many years
It contained all my secrets
My hope and my fears

I wanted to reach out
And hold that girl tight
Then tell her that everything
Would eventually be alright

Even if I could tell her
She already knew back then
The world was a cruel place
She'd never be okay again

She fell in love too easily
She just wanted to feel
That somebody might want her
Even if that seemed surreal

So many times already
She'd been led to believe
That nobody could love her
Something she could never conceive

She thought she wasn't worthy
Even her own mother told her so
Too scruffy and too fat
Who would stoop so low?

Even though she was clever
In a test got a straight A
Only second in the class
Not good enough on that day

The sadness and the loneliness
She generally did feel
Felt heart wrenching to read
And so incredibly real

No-one to confide in
She had nowhere to turn
Her emotions hidden deeply
Continued to fiercely burn

Sadly, she was vulnerable
Believed the things she heard
Surely a mother wouldn't lie
So, she believed every word

I wish I could tell her now
That she was perfectly okay
Good enough at that time
In every single way

Maybe remarks could be ignored
Be water off a ducks back
Though I sincerely doubt it
Her mother had the knack

The attacks were never direct
Implied and insinuated
If the girl dared fight back
They were denied and repudiated

Nothing could ever be proved
That would never be allowed
She only wants to change you
Because then could she be proud

So the story ends
In emotional distress
and lifelong upset
You're still such a mess

Even though her Mum died
A little time ago
The feelings of distress
Don't seem to smaller grow

You thought they'd die with her
That you'd feel some release
They feel ever more complicated
And never appear to cease

Ghosts of the past remain
Will it always be that way?
Forever there to haunt you
Until your dying day

Where Did She Go?

Where did she go?
The girl who loved 'no fear'
Posters on her walls
Of the motto she held dear

Don't let your fear
Get in the way of your dreams
She lived by that motto
Constantly searching for extremes

She used to be carefree
Just in search of some fun
Weekends spent on camping trips
Defying the will of her mum

She drove an orange beetle
Oh, how she loved that car
Her first taste of freedom
Allowed her to travel afar

She wore a leather jacket
Had dyed bright orange hair
What other people thought
She simply didn't care

Skydived out of a plane
Just for the sheer thrill
Loved the adrenaline high
Better than any pill

Partied out in night clubs
Danced upon the stage
Nobody back then
Ever put her in a cage

Utterly lost in the music
She just didn't care
What anyone else thought
Or if they did stare

She'd walk home late at night
In the dark and all alone
She was never afraid
She was not fear prone

Like a ghost she's disappeared
Don't know where she went
But I feel grief that she's gone
Emptiness and malcontent

The girl that's replaced her
Her motto's 'fear everything '
It's so all consuming
Totally absorbing

She's scared to be alone
Without someone by her side
Meeting new people creates anxiety
Which feels so hard to abide

She's scared of her son
And the damage he inflicts
The alcohol that she drinks
And how so soon it addicts

She fears going to work
Doesn't feel fit to do her job
What if she's forgotten everything?
Can't hack it and starts to sob

Even supermarkets make her panic
Impossible to explain why
Why does it now seem so hard
To get the shopping supply?

She's scared of the future
Fearful of the next day
Petrified of being rejected
That her loved ones just won't stay

Often, I long to be that girl
The one who was happy and free
But now feel resigned that she
Will never come back to me

Weight

I see myself as fat
When others say I'm "thin"
Why don't I feel happy?
Within my own skin

When did it all start?
Was it when I was small?
Then, I ate for comfort
As I had no friends at all

I started to get bigger
And rather overweight
I didn't like my body
Had loathing and self hate

School kids called me blubber
Or sometimes fatso too
The names were so cruel
And made me feel so blue

Other upsetting comments
Were 'she's got such fat legs'
Girls forced to wear skirts
Trousers weren't in the regs

I'd "never get a boyfriend"
That's what my mum said
I totally believed it
And it stuck in my head

Whilst minding my own business
One day walking through town
Two girls, older than me
Looked at me with a frown

Gosh, "Look at her belly"
Don't you think "she is fat?"
"I wouldn't wear those jeans"
"If I looked like that"

My best friend was pretty
Everyone thought she was fit
And all the teenage boys
Wanted to get in her kit

I just wanted someone
To look at me that way
I longed to feel attractive
Even if only for one day

She got all the boyfriends
Seemed my mum was right
If they glanced at me
I felt they couldn't stand the sight

My mum was a feeder
And I liked to eat
She worked in the school kitchen
That seemed pretty neat

I'd tell her I was hungry
And she'd give food to me
A burger, or a bun
Or maybe a Crunchie

If I had a test at school
She'd give me a chocolate bar
"Make sure you eat this first
And then you will go far"

Apparently "it's brain food"
Or so that's what she'd read
Of course, I knew no better
So, I believed what she said

Tests were normally morning
I'd hide it in my coat
I wasn't at all hungry
But I'd force it down my throat

I'd only just had breakfast
But I wanted to succeed
I had to pass the test
My mum's approval I did need

But then, she took me to “fat club”
For weigh ins every week
In a room full of strangers
I felt ashamed of my physique

I begged not to go
I definitely wasn’t keen
I shouldn’t ever have been there
I was only about thirteen

The rest of the people there
Were all middle age
I didn’t fit in with them
I felt trapped in a cage

I would wait for my turn
The leader called out my name
Then stand on the scales
Inside dying of shame

Standing completely still
And breathing deeply in
Wishing that my body
Was just really thin

My weight stayed the same
Pounds didn’t come off
As when no one was looking
I’d continue to scoff

I just felt a failure
I'd keep my tears inside
Going there each week
Was shattering my pride

They discussed eating weekly
What foods were considered bad
Then, we had to confess
To those that we'd had

I still retain the scars
Etched on my heart
Desperately wanting to heal
Not knowing where to start

Some clothes still feel difficult
When them I try to wear
I feel very self-conscious
Although, I try not to care

Years later, I've lost weight
I have less belly to hide
But still despite this
I feel like the fat girl inside

Is it possible that one day
I will stand on this earth
And not feel my weight
Is linked to my worth?

Coming Out

The first time I told someone
I was shaking so much inside
My palms were hot and sweaty
I just wanted to run and hide

I was nauseous and shaky
And felt my heart intensely racing
Restless became my legs
And I was unable to stop pacing

My anti-depressants had changed
And made it impossible to control my urge
They drove my appetite wild
Increasing my need to binge and purge

Therefore, after more than 20 years
Of the secret I'd kept locked away
I became aware I had no choice
I finally had to say

So, I told my general practitioner
He was understanding and so kind
Filled with panic and instant regret
As, I realised I couldn't press rewind

"Please don't write it down!"
"I don't want anyone else to know"
Not sure I could stand the way
That others might look at me so

I've kept it hidden so completely
My husband, I have never even told him
I'm scared, ashamed and embarrassed
My secret is too frightful and grim

I predict what others would say
"How can she make herself sick?"
"Why on earth would she do it?"
"Does it give her some sort of kick?"

It's so "degrading and disgusting"
Someone can "do something like that"
She's been "reading too many magazines"
Is impressionable and "doesn't want to get fat"

If your food intake is restricted
They'll say "Just have more to eat!"
My thoughts tell me people would judge me
It's obvious, this thing she could beat

She must be "doing it for attention"
She clearly "chooses to do it
How selfish to put her family through it
Surely otherwise she would just quit

I dread the whispers of people knowing
The looks that they give to you
Their eyes say “She should be ashamed”
But it’s too late! “We all know what you do”

Feeling Violated

I know you needed to tell someone
But why did it have to be her?
I know she's your sister
So, I don't want to cause a stir

But we've never been that close
We're just not the same
But you've told her my secret
I feel so full of shame

You said I've got an issue
That I don't eat enough
Sometimes, I make myself vomit
And all the other stuff

I've never told my friends
I don't want them to know
The chasm that's between us
Continues to grow and grow

But now the truth is out
It cannot be erased
What if she tells others?
Suddenly I feel I'm stuck in a maze

I'm lost, there's no way out
I've got no control at all
Every way that I turn
Feels like I hit a wall

Like a rabbit in the headlights
I feel irrational fear
It seems completely illogical
About the secret I held dear

I feel so violated
My secret you just gave away
Did my feelings not matter?
To you at all on that day

I know things are hard for you
But, that secret was mine
I'm not sure how to get over it
And go back to being fine

You are not just my husband
You are my best friend
But now you've lost my trust
I don't know how we can mend

All of a sudden, I feel all alone
Without you by my side
Who else in the world
In my secrets can I confide

It might seem minor to you
But I feel stabbed though the heart
I'm so tired now of fighting
I want this pain to depart

Sometimes I wish the world
Would open up and swallow me
Life would be much easier
Everyone could go back to being happy

Conflicting Emotions

It been a couple of years
Since the day my mother died
Emotions vast and complex
So many tears I have cried

My feelings for her are conflicted
Not just love and sense of grief
There's also anger and resentment
And a partial sense of relief

Though, at the end of the day
She was still my Mum
When I nursed her as she was dying
Love was the emotion that won

Sometimes I feel that inside
There are two versions of me
There's the eight year old girl
And the adult with a uni degree

The little girl deep within
Loved her with all her heart
Feels an enormous hole was left
When from this earth she did depart

The only thing she ever wanted
Was her Mum to love her and be proud
Although her Mum told her she loved her
The other word was never uttered aloud

It's too late now her Mum is gone
And the little girl will never know
Did her Mum feel proud of her?
Or did she never feel so?

Is it wrong that there's part of me
That's relieved now she's not on this earth?
Because she can no longer criticise
And continue to affect my worth

I want to protect my daughter
She's self-conscious like a normal teen
She reminds me of myself at that age
When comments started to get mean

I'm glad she'll never be exposed
To the disapproving comments that I had
That made me feel never good enough
And that my Mum thought I was bad

She frequently told me I was fat
I'd be better if I could lose weight
If we argued and I got angry
She told me no one would ever like that trait

She never like me having freedom
She controlled many things that I did
Only if she approved could I go out
Unless I lied she would forbid

So, I'm glad my daughter won't hear
That she has "put on some weight"
Or should have "done better in a test"
Or looks" terrible and a complete state"

Confusingly, part of me misses her
And despite all the bad
Sometimes I wish I could phone her
To tell her any news which I had

But conflicting co-existing emotions
Are deeply difficult to bear
Bewilderingly, I can't comprehend
What possibly is going on inside there

How can you feel both these things
Polar opposites for the same person?
The more my brain tries to rationalise it
The more my confusion does worsen

Filled with so much self-guilt
How can I think ill of the dead?
Why can't I let bygones be bygones
And forget every hurtful thing she said?

That feels like an impossible task
When it's left such a lasting scar
Regrettably I still feel resentment
She continues to affect me from afar

Maybe it wasn't entirely her fault
Perhaps, she'd been criticised too
When she was young and impressionable
So that was the only way she knew

Was it her way of showing love?
Was she emotionally neglected as a child?
Or was I just terrible as a youngster
Was the problem with me, Was I wild?

It just doesn't seem to get easier
Memories, still cause so much pain
The chance to resolve conflict lost forever
As she's gone, I will never see her again!

Parent Child Reversal

I am the parent
Of that I am sure
I remember his birth
It was him that I bore

But something has changed
Authority no more
I am not the parent
Not like before

The power has shifted
He's stronger and bigger
With a volatile temper
That anything could trigger

I'm like the scared child
And he's the angry Dad
When will he erupt?
When will he get mad?

Will it just be shouting?
Right in my face
Makes me anxious inside
Even if that's the case

Or slamming of doors
And stomping about
Maybe things will be thrown
As the pressure does mount

Whatever he can find
That is near to his hand
A pen pot, a glass holder
A rock, always unplanned

Sometimes he will smash things
If there's nothing to throw
Like a light switch or plate
What havoc he does bestow

I've hidden in the bedroom
Put the lock on the door
But he can break through it.
It's not strong enough anymore

At times you are barged
Pushed into a wall
Perhaps you will stumble
Even worse, take a fall

Before he might hit
But was never sustained
Until recently he was small
So could be contained

Rapidly he is growing
One attack left me scared
How could you do that?
To someone if you cared

I'd gone for some space
Aware he was getting cross
Followed closely behind
Trapped, I was at a loss

A drink smashed on the floor
Exasperated and drained
I turned away from him
And on my back punches rained

Three in the centre
I turned to see his face
Full of anger and hatred
No love in this case

Struck three more times
On the front of my chest
Unable to fight back
Frozen, body too stressed

The line has now been crossed
I can never go back
I'm living in fear
Might there be another attack?

Everything I look at
I now have to think
Is it really safe to leave
A knife drying by the sink?

What if he gets angry?
Could that be what he'd grab?
Would he stop himself?
Or in anger may he stab?

So now when I hear him
Starting to get mad
I hide like a scared child
Behind the sofa, feeling sad

It's hard to keep living
Like this each day
Wanting to escape
Knowing there's no way

There are so many services
For children who are abused
But parents fear their children?
You must be confused

It feels there's nowhere at all
For parents to turn
It seems you don't exist
You are no-one's concern

Bodyguard

I am sitting in the bedroom
Beside me, my husband's still asleep
I'm too scared to go downstairs
So close to him I keep

I'm safe when I am near him
He's now my bodyguard
I know that he'll protect me
Not let anyone hit me hard

So, I hide close there beside him
Don't want to leave his side
Afraid to venture out alone
Therefore, I'll continue to hide

Only if my child's in his room
Do I feel sure that I can try
To sneak downstairs to get a drink
Quietly past his room tip toeing by

Nervously, I leave my prison cell
I hope that he doesn't hear me
I cannot disturb the sleeping beast
As then I would have to quickly flee

Gladly, I safely make it back
Filled with enormous relief
All this stress just for a coffee
Inside I feel so full of grief

Harbour Walls

Multiple courses have been attended
Aimed to make a better parent of me
There are plenty of different strategies
It's just not quite so easy

Having a child with special needs
Meltdowns frequent and out of the blue
Nothing in life is straight forward
When there's challenging behaviour too

The analogy is you're the harbour walls
And your child is like the boat
If the storm outside is raging
The ship might be struggling to stay afloat

The harbour walls will remain steadfast
Calm waters inside, despite the storm
Helps your child to feel safe
To regulate and start to conform

It's fine when storms are infrequent
Quickly over, don't last that long
But when it seems they rage for ever
Impossible for the walls to stay strong

The harbour walls start growing weak
Showing signs of wear and tear
Visible cracks appear and grow deeper
There's an urgent need of repair

While the sea is turbulent and violent
How can repairs ever get underway?
It needs a spell of calmer weather
But the storm clouds just seem to stay

Fragile, the harbour now is crumbling
Grave danger of being destroyed
But the cavalry isn't coming
There's no back up that's being deployed

How do you repair your strength as a parent?
Apparently, with an abundance of self-care
Though, when feeling low or overwhelmed
It's hard to find motivation or time to spare

Often I long not to be those walls
That I had a nice calm stretch of sea
Not always worried about the next storm
Or quite how threatening it will be

Magic Wand

I wish that I could change
Everything for you
Wave a magic wand
Stop what you're going through

I'd take away your pain
Make your sadness go away
It so breaks my heart
When I see you this way

I'd brighten the skies above
Create rainbows up high
Put a smile upon your face
Make you no longer want to cry

I'd eliminate the loneliness
And anxiety that you feel
Somehow, I'd make your life
Seem much less of an ordeal

Remove your separation anxiety
Thinking bad things will take place
Each time your away from family
Panic! Your heart then starts to race

I stop you needing to swallow
The many tablets that you do
That help you to concentrate
And your fidgetiness to subdue

I'd make your peers accepting
So you wouldn't be excluded
Though, you might be a bit different
You are desperate to be included

I'd give you contentment
With whatever things you had
I'd lessen your irritability
So you didn't always feel mad

You'd not compare yourself to others
And constantly feel hard done
Finally, you would enjoy yourself
Maybe even have some fun

You wouldn't need reassurance
Because your self-esteem is so low
You would feel proud of your self
And your confidence would show

You'd be able to realise your worth
How you're a bright shining star
Your self-doubt would be no longer
You'd believe how loved you are

If only I had that wand
I could make everything alright
I could change the course of time
And make your future look so bright

Respite

(Written after a respite stay with friends in a static caravan run by Social services and Action for Children for carers to have a break away from family)

I'd like to stay here forever
In this secret escape
Where life feels so very different
You can shed your carer's cape

Everything is so quiet
And there's a feeling of peace
Hard to recall the last time
I felt such a stress release

Sitting listening to nature
Or reading a book in the sun
Time spent chatting with friends
Even some moments of fun

There is no fighting or yelling
No constant shadow by your side
Gone for a little while
Is my desire to run and hide

No pressure to do anything
On the endless list of stuff to do
Not just normal household chores
There's all the extra stuff too

So many emails with school
Various forms to fill in
Different services involved
It's hard to know where to begin

Medical appointments to organise
Various meetings to attend
Prescriptions to collect
Feels the jobs never end

But for a few days
That simply magically disappears
You somehow feel lighter
For once not drowning in tears

You're reminded of the good things
That can be present in life
Your batteries start to recharge
Before you return to face the strife

Maybe in the tough moments
You might feel a little hope
That there's still joy to be had
And respite to help you cope

This is Who I Am!

Astonishingly, I no longer want to hide
My unspeakable secrets anymore
I'm aware that once they're out
It can never go back to before

I've been terrified of people discovering
For as long as I can recall
But now I'm making a choice
I won't let them make me feel small

I'm no longer scared of their reaction
That they might think less of me
I'm so tired of keeping this secret
Will no longer let hiding sap my energy

I don't want for them to judge me
Or look at me in horror or dismay
Though I'm probably my biggest judge
And my own worst critic, anyway

I don't want any unwelcome advice
Good intentioned, trying to change me
I want to be accepted as I am
I certainly don't need any pity

I will work to fight against stigma
Refuse any longer to feel ashamed
I know it that it isn't my fault
No more will I accept feeling blamed

The people who do really matter
Faithful true friends will still be there
I know that they will support me
It's only their opinion for which I do care

Finally, I am choosing to be strong
Share the truth for all to see
Not just the good but also my flaws
This is who I am, in my entirety!

www.ingramcontent.com/pod-product-compliance
Lightning Source LLC
Chambersburg PA
CBHW051734130826
49812CB00033B/853
9789357211864